PSID and BOLTER

Carolyn Bear

Illustrated by
Peter Cottrill

OXFORD

OXFORD
UNIVERSITY PRESS

Great Clarendon Street, Oxford OX2 6DP

Oxford University Press is a department of the University of Oxford.
It furthers the University's objective of excellence in research, scholarship,
and education by publishing worldwide in

Oxford New York

Auckland Bangkok Buenos Aires Cape Town Chennai
Dar es Salaam Delhi Hong Kong Istanbul Karachi Kolkata
Kuala Lumpur Madrid Melbourne Mexico City Mumbai Nairobi
São Paulo Shanghai Taipei Tokyo Toronto

with an associated company in Berlin

Oxford is a registered trade mark of Oxford University Press
in the UK and in certain other countries

British Library Cataloguing in Publication Data

Data available

ISBN 0 19 919493 9

1 3 5 7 9 10 8 6 4 2

Guided Reading Pack (6 of the same title): ISBN 0 19 919572 2
Mixed Pack (1 of 6 different titles): ISBN 0 19 919499 8
Class Pack (6 copies of 6 titles): ISBN 0 19 919500 5

Printed in Hong Kong

Contents

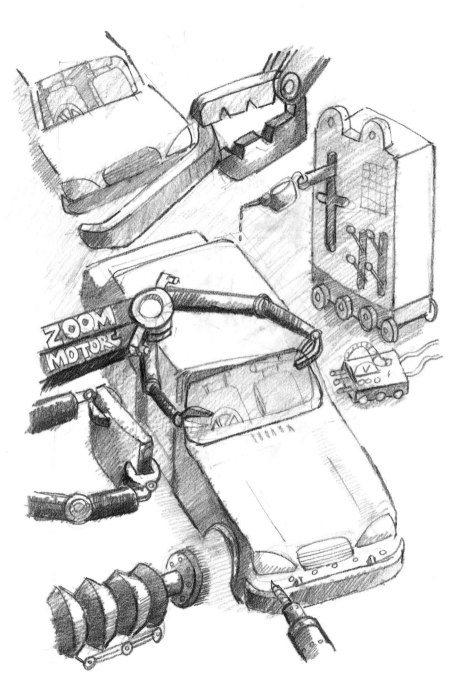

Chapter 1

Keep Clear! Robots at Work

Psid and Bolter worked in a car factory.

Inside this factory there was a line of robots more than a mile long. There were huge ones that went CLUNK... CLUNK... CLUNK...

There were fierce looking ones with loads of jagged teeth that went SNIP... SNAP... CRUNCH. And there were tall, thin, wiry ones. They had arms that could twist and twiddle, and fix even the tiniest pieces in place.

The cars moved along the line from robot to robot, until at the very end, they were ready to go out on the road.

Psid and Bolter were the very last robots on the line.

Psid's job was to add the Go Faster stripes.

He started at one end of each car and went "PsssssssssssiD", right down to the other end.

He left a long, straight, beautiful stripe of red.

Then he'd go "PssssssssssssiD" again and leave a second, beautiful, straight stripe of white.

Bolter's job was to check and double-check the bolts on the wheels.

He worked with a gentle: "Brrrrrrr"…"Brrrrrrr"…"Brrrrrrr"…"Brrrrrrr" noise. Four times on each wheel, four wheels on each car.

Psid and Bolter were very proud of their jobs. It was an important place to be, on the end of the line.

Chapter 2

A New Boss

Then one day, the factory got a new
Boss. He was a tall man with big, bushy
eyebrows. He walked up and down the
line, followed by a team of men. They
were checking the robots at work.

They stopped beside Psid and Bolter.

"Pssssssssid," went Psid proudly,
painting a red stripe. Then "Psssssssid"
again, proudly painting a white one.

"Brrrrrrr"… "Brrrrrrr"…"Brrrrrrr"…
"Brrrrrrr," went Bolter, loudly and busily.

Psid stood back, expecting praise. Bolter paused, hoping for a pat on the back. But then they could hardly believe their ears.

The Boss was glaring at them from under his bushy eyebrows.

"It won't do," he said. "You'll have to work faster. This factory has to make ten more cars a day."

That's when the trouble started.

Each day, cars started coming down the line faster and faster.

All the robots were grumbling and groaning, creaking and moaning, and getting in each other's way. Psid and Bolter could hardly keep up.

The robots worked at twice their normal speed, non-stop, round-the-clock, for more than three weeks.

Then, one night, disaster struck.

A worker who checked the cars as they left the factory, suddenly noticed PINK Go Faster stripes!

And the worker who stood next to him saw a car with WHEEL WOBBLE!

The Boss was woken up and brought out of his bed to see this terrible sight with his own eyes.

"STOP THE LINE!" he roared.

The robots slowed down and, at last, the line ground to a standstill. A terrible silence fell over the factory.

The Boss and his team walked down the line checking the work of each robot in turn.

They got closer and closer to Psid and Bolter. Then they stopped.

"It's clear who's to blame," said the Boss.

Psid and Bolter hung their heads.

"Back to work, lads," the Boss said to the other robots.

Psid and Bolter started to slide back to their places. They felt very ashamed of themselves.

"Not you," said the Boss. "You two are coming with me."

The two of them were led in disgrace past the entire line of robots.

They were left in a store room at the very edge of the factory. It was full of old sandwich papers and empty cola cans.

This was the place where robots who were broken, or simply too old to do their job properly, were left to rust away.

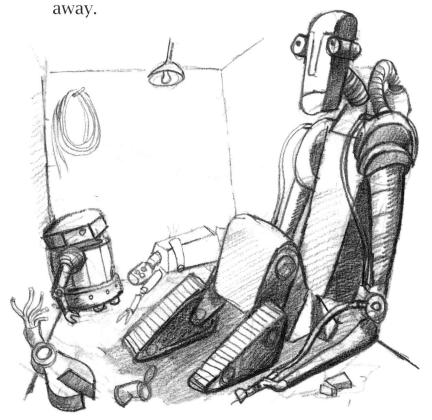

Chapter 3

The Escape

Psid was standing in a dark corner of the store room. He was listening sadly to the busy hum of the robots working on the line outside.

"Brrrrrrrrr," said Bolter. "It's cold in here."

"If only we could esssscape..." said Psid.

The two of them stared at the big, bolted doors that stood between them and the outside world.

Then Psid had an idea.

"Pssssst, Bolter!" he said. "If you can do up bolts, ssssssurely you can *un*-do them?"

The very idea of undoing bolts went against everything Bolter had ever learned.

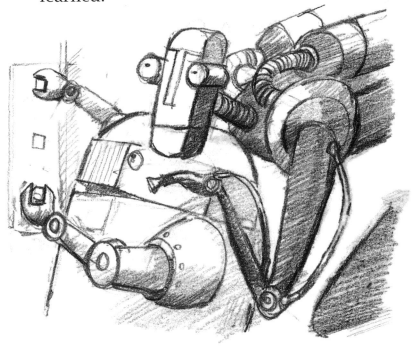

"*Un*-do them?" he said, doubtfully.

"Yesssssss," said Psid.

"But I'm a bolter, not an un-bolter," said Bolter.

"But Bolter, you're so strong and so clever, it should be ssssimple for you."

"I suppose I could try," said Bolter.

He rolled over to the door and went "rrrrrrB"… "rrrrrrrB" …"rrrrrrrB" …"rrrrrrrB".

And before their very eyes, the doors swung open.

There was the outside world.

There was the car park. There were all the gleaming brand new cars, waiting in neat rows to be taken away to their owners. There were the great long car transporters waiting to deliver them.

And there was the road that led out through the factory gates...

The two of them rumbled along between tall factory buildings. The gates were locked. But that wasn't a problem.

"rrrrrB"… "rrrrrrB" …"rrrrrrB"
…"rrrrrrB." Bolter had them off their
hinges in no time at all.

So Psid and Bolter got away.

Chapter 4

A Strange Sight in the Night

The two strange figures glided off along silent roads. In the houses on either side, everyone was fast asleep.

Everyone, that is, apart from one old lady. She had got up in the middle of the night to make a cup of cocoa.

Looking out of the kitchen window, she had the shock of her life.

She dialled 999, right away.

"Aliens," she said. "Or maybe they were dinosaurs. I saw them, clear as daylight. Two of them. They were going down Maple Grove."

The police sent a squad car.

By the time they arrived, the old lady's husband and their next-door neighbours and the people next door to them were all waiting on the pavement.

"They went that way…" they said, pointing out of town.

The policemen didn't really believe they'd seen aliens, let alone dinosaurs. But to keep everyone happy, they examined the tracks on the road with their torches.

They could see that some very strange creatures indeed had passed that way.

So the policemen started up their siren, and with their blue light flashing, the police car went chasing off into the night.

Psid and Bolter heard the police car coming. They hid behind a large signboard and waited, nervously.

They heard the police car screech to a halt.

"Pssssst," whispered Psid to Bolter. "What shall we do now? If they find us, they'll take us back to the factory."

"Leave it to me," said Bolter. The policemen were still busy searching down the road with their torches.

Bolter crept up to their car.

Psid heard: "rrrrrrB"… "rrrrrrrB" …"rrrrrrrB" …"rrrrrrrB", four times, coming through the darkness.

"Now, let's make a dash for it," said Bolter.

The two robots headed off down the road at full speed.

"There they are!" shouted a policeman. He leapt into the police car and started up the engine.

But it didn't get very far.

Psid and Bolter were soon out of town and in the open countryside.

They had never been anywhere so big or so empty before.

Cows in the fields woke up and watched as they passed. Sheep huddled together for safety and then ran all round their field in a frightened bunch.

It wasn't long before more police cars were sent after the runaway robots. Psid and Bolter could hear their sirens in the distance.

They reached a crossroads. They didn't know which way to go. Then Bolter had another idea.

"You can spray paint, Psid," he said. "Get to work."

Now, for a robot who'd only ever painted Go Faster stripes, Psid did a very good job.

Psid and Bolter turned left and headed away into the countryside.

All the police cars turned right. They ended up back in town.

The two robots made their way slowly, bit by bit, up a hill.

Then they went down the other side, very fast indeed.

As the night wore on, both of them started feeling very tired.

Psid and Bolter were factory robots. They weren't designed for running about on roads. Psid could feel his wheels wearing thin. And Bolter could feel his joints coming loose.

At last, they came to a little wood.

"Oh, look," said Psid, who had
never seen a wood before. "Look at
all those lamp posts in the middle of
nowhere. Let's hide between them and
have a rest."

So Psid and Bolter left the road and
settled down on a big, soft bed of
leaves.

It was very dark and very quiet in
the wood.

Neither Psid nor Bolter had ever been anywhere so quiet, and in the quietness they kept hearing noises. There was a rustle and then something went "WOOOOOO".

Psid huddled closer to Bolter. All around, they could see little yellow eyes glinting in the darkness.

"Brrrrrrrr." Bolter's teeth were chattering with fear.

Then "the something" went "WOOOOOO", again.

And then it went "TOOWIT –
TOOWOOOO", right beside them.

"That's it," said Bolter. "I'm off!"

He started to make his way as
fast as he could, through the wood.

Psid followed close behind him.
That's when they saw "IT".

"IT" was huge. Much bigger than
Psid. Much bigger than Bolter. "IT"
stood with its huge, jagged teeth
outlined against the sky.

Bolter and Psid stood there, frozen
with terror.

34

Chapter 5

Save our Wood

Dawn was breaking in a thin line of pink on the horizon. Birds started to sing and everything began to look less scary.

As the sun came up, Psid and Bolter saw what "IT" was.

It was only a big mechanical digger. Underneath "IT" was a boy lying in a sleeping bag, fast asleep. The boy had a handwritten sign which said: *SAVE OUR WOOD.*

Psid and Bolter had never seen a boy before. They didn't know that people could be so small. They crept closer to have a better look.

The boy opened his eyes.

He saw two robots standing over him.

He leapt out of the sleeping bag and shouted, "No! You can't do it! You can't build a road through our wood!"

Psid looked at Bolter and Bolter
looked at Psid.

"No," said Bolter. "You're right. We
can't."

"We're from a car factory, you
sssseeee," said Psid. "We build cars,
not roads."

The boy rubbed his eyes and looked
more closely.

"What *can* you do then?" he asked.

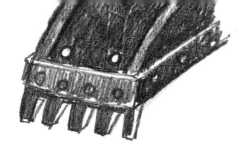

Bolter explained that he was very good at taking things apart and putting them together again. Psid told the boy how he could paint anything as long as it was red or white or pink.

That's when the boy explained about the digger.

That very morning, road workers were coming to build a motorway right through the middle of the wood.

"There are no houses here, you see," said the boy. "So there are no people living here to complain. But it's home to lots and lots of animals…"

Some small creatures crept out of hiding.

They were the ones who had been making all the rustling and "WOOOO" noises that had frightened Psid and Bolter in the night.

They looked at Psid and Bolter
hopefully.

Bolter looked at Psid and Psid looked
at Bolter.

"Right, lad," said Bolter. "Let's get to
work."

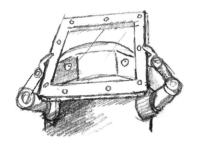

Chapter 6

A House from Nowhere

The road builders arrived later that morning. They couldn't find their mechanical digger anywhere.

In its place stood the most amazing house.

It had red and white windows of a strange shape and a little pink door. It had a roof made of rubber tiles and it had red and white and pink roses painted all around the doorway.

The road builders telephoned their office. Before very long, a lot more people arrived. They stood in a big crowd, looking at the house.

Then they argued about what should
be done about it.

"Pull it down!"

"Move it!"

"Blow it up!"

A man rode up on a bicycle. He was
bald with a beard and he looked
important.

He said, "That's not a house."

Everyone stopped and looked
around.

"That's not a house," he repeated.

People stared at him as if he were mad.

"That's not a house," he said. "That's a work of Art. I'm going to make sure that it stays right where it is. No one is going to build a road through this wood."

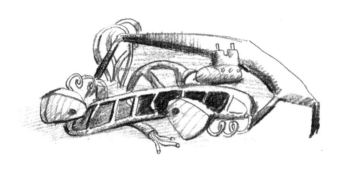

Chapter 7

Faster and Faster!

Meanwhile, back at the car factory, the other robots on the line were having to work faster than ever. And they didn't have Psid and Bolter to help.

The Boss with the bushy eyebrows stood at the gates. He had a wide grin on his face. He was counting the bright, new shiny cars as they left the factory.

But inside the factory, there were sounds of creaking and groaning.

The robots were forced to CLUNK-CLUNK-CLUNK...SNIP-SNAP SNIP... CRUNCH-CRUNCH-CRUNCH at an almost impossible speed.

Sometimes there was a horrible screech as one of them ran out of oil.

The robot who was trying to do Psid's job started to shake as he sprayed on the stripes. And the one who stood in Bolter's place could hardly keep up.

Nobody noticed the problems at first. The faults in the new cars were so tiny. Just a bolt missing here. Or a nut missing there.

Or a little wobble in the Go Faster stripes.

"Faster!" ordered the Boss. "You can do better than this. I want twenty more cars a day!"

The robots did their best to keep up, but they kept making mistakes. Some cars were going down the line so fast that they didn't get any Go Faster stripes. Some of their bolts were so loose they were falling off.

Then the most terrible thing happened.

A car went so fast down the line that it had no bolts at all. As it left the factory, it fell into fifty pieces at the Boss's feet.

"STOP THE LINE!" yelled the Boss. "What's going on?"

The robots came to a halt with a hiss and a groan and a sigh.

They didn't dare say anything.

"Come on," said the Boss, glaring under his eyebrows. "Speak up!"

The robots huddled together and hung their heads. Then the oldest robot creaked to the front.

"If…" he said, nervously.

"Yes?" said the Boss.

"If only…" the robot said.

"If only WHAT?" snapped the Boss.

"If only there were more of us. Then we could keep up."

Another robot shouted, "Bring back Psid and Bolter!"

Then a third robot cried, "We're not making another car until Psid and Bolter are back in the line."

They all started CLUNKING and CRUNCHING and SNIPPING and SNAPPING. They stamped on the ground and banged on the bench.

The Boss frowned so hard that his bushy eyebrows met in the middle. He scratched his chin and thought about this. And he made up his mind very quickly indeed.

"Very well," he said. "We'll give them another chance."

All the robots hooted and cheered. They said things like, "Hip-hip-hip for Psid", and "Bully for Bolter!"

Someone went to fetch them from the storeroom.

But of course, Psid and Bolter weren't there.

"Where are they?" stormed the Boss. But no one knew.

Chapter 8

No Place for a Robot

In the house in the wood, Psid and Bolter were not happy. The boy had gone home with his parents. Now it was damp and cold and lonely.

Psid and Bolter huddled together. They missed the other robots. They missed the warm factory and the friendly clatter of noise.

Psid's teeth chattered and he was afraid of going rusty. Bolter's joints were stiff because they hadn't been oiled. The wood was fine for animals and birds to live in. But it was no place for a robot.

"I wish we could go home," said Psid.

Chapter 9

The Boss has a Surprise

That evening, the Boss went home early. He felt cross and he had a headache. He'd had such a bad day at the factory. As he drove past the wood, he slowed down and decided he would stop for a breath of fresh air. He'd never had time to stop before.

That's when he saw the strange house in the wood.

There was something very odd about it. He went to take a closer look.

It reminded him of something.

What an odd chimney it had! And he'd never seen a roof that looked quite like that before.

Inside the house, Psid spotted the Boss walking towards them.

"Pssst!" he said to Bolter. "Look who it issss!"

The Boss opened the door. He didn't see the robots, but Bolter started to shake with fright.

He dropped a bolt he was holding. It rolled towards the Boss' feet.

"Who's there?" yelled the Boss, looking around.

But he couldn't see anyone.

Then he looked around and got the shock of his life. There were Psid and Bolter, staring at him.

"What are you doing in this house?" he asked.

Bolter drew himself up to his full height. "This is our house. We built it."

"*You* built it!" said the Boss. He looked around. How well it was made. How strong and how well bolted together it was. How fine the painted roses were, all around the windows.

"I'd like to take you back, lads," he said. "What do you say?"

Psid looked at Bolter and Bolter looked at Psid. They wanted to go back to the factory, but they were too proud to say so.

It took the Boss half an hour to persuade them to come back to work.

Chapter 10
Back on the Line

Next day, Psid and Bolter went back to the factory in a blaze of glory. All the other robots stood to attention and honked the horns of the cars to celebrate. The two of them slid back to their places on the line.

So that was the end of all the troubles at the factory. The Boss never made any of the robots work faster than Psid and Bolter could work, and they hardly ever made mistakes.

The bright, new shiny cars rolled off the line, one by one. The great big transporters drove off around the country to deliver them.

Psid and Bolter had shown how clever they were at thinking up new ideas. So now and again, the Boss let them suggest new ways to make the cars even better.

About the author

When I was at school I wanted to become an inventor. But in order to invent things you have to be good at maths. And I wasn't. So I invented stories instead.

I hope you'll enjoy reading about Psid and Bolter, the two robots I've invented specially for this story.